BENJAMIN BRITTEN

Moderato & Nocturne

from Sonatina Romantica (1940)
for solo piano

FABER *ff* MUSIC

© 1986 by Faber Music Ltd
First published in 1986 by Faber Music Ltd
3 Queen Square London WC1N 3AU
Music drawn by Lincoln Castle Music
Cover design by S & M Tucker
Printed in England by Caligraving Ltd
All rights reserved

ISBN 0-571-50878-2

Duration: 7 minutes

To buy Faber Music publications or to find out about the full range of titles available
please contact your local retailer or Faber Music sales enquiries:

Faber Music Ltd, Burnt Mill, Elizabeth Way, Harlow, Essex CM20 2HX
Tel: +44 (0)1279 82 89 82   Fax: +44 (0)1279 82 89 83
Email: sales@fabermusic.com   www.fabermusic.com

When George Benjamin gave the first performance of the *Sonatina Romantica* at the Aldeburgh Festival on 16 June 1983, Sir Peter Pears contributed the following note to the programme book:

> 'During our stay in America in the early years of the war, Ben and I lived for much of the time with Elizabeth and William Mayer in Amityville. Dr Mayer was the Senior Neurologist at the Long Island Home, the Director of which was Dr William B Titley. In 1940 Ben interrupted work on the *Sinfonia da Requiem* to compose this little *Sonatina* for Titley, who was a keen amateur pianist. He had been struggling with the *Invitation to the Waltz* and Ben presented the *Sonatina Romantica* as a tactful suggestion that he change his tune! But the doctor, I seem to remember, remained determined to master Weber!'

The *Sonatina* was in four movements: 'Moderato ma drammatico', 'Nocturne: Andante', 'Burlesque: Allegro con fuoco', and 'Toccata: Presto possibile', and Britten completed all four movements. Manuscripts in the possession of the Britten–Pears Library at Aldeburgh show that the composer was dissatisfied with the finale and embarked on a revision of it. It was while he was working on this revision that he must have decided to abandon the *Sonatina*; the revision was left unfinished and he made it known that the *Sonatina* was among the works he rejected.

The composer's Trustees share his doubts about the finale (which is excluded from this edition) but feel that the first two movements have character and charm and, in particular, could play a very useful role as teaching pieces, thus fulfilling at least part of the composer's original intention. There is so little of Britten's for solo piano that music of quality for the instrument should not be left to languish unpublished. The 'Burlesque', the third movement, is too short to make sense in the present context. The publishers will hope to find a place for it in a future collection of shorter teaching pieces.

The 'Moderato' and 'Nocturne' have been edited and seen through the press by Colin Matthews.

Donald Mitchell

MODERATO

from Sonatina Romantica

BENJAMIN BRITTEN
(1913–1976)

4

NOCTURNE
from Sonatina Romantica

Ped. al fine